T0365856

He who knows
others is
learned: he who
knows himself
is wise.

—Lao-Tzu Tao
Te Ching

Not until we are
lost do we begin
to understand
ourselves.

—Henry David
Thoreau

No one
remains quite
what he/she
was when he/
she recognized
themselves.

—Thomas Mann

One's own self is well hidden from one's own self. Of all mines of treasure, one's own is the last to be dug up.

—Friedrich Nietzsche

Know thyself, and thou shall know the universe and God.

—Quote from the Temple of Apollo

We learn to see ourselves in relation to all other creatures.

—Pope Francis

I GOTTA TELL GRANDPA

A Story and Workbook about Finding and Being Yourself

Jay Steineckert, LCSW

This is a storybook and a workbook about
finding and growing up with your own self-identity.
This book is for kids everywhere
and for adults who sometimes
wonder who they are.
The search for the true self
is the greatest search of all.

This storybook has an awesome and fun song called
"Will You Ever Grow Up?"

You can download this mp3 song for free when you
purchase this book by going to: Igottatellgrandpa.com,
Or by buying the electronic version of this book
on Amazon.com, etc.

The lyrics to the song and the download code are found on page 42 of this book.

Archway Publishing books may be ordered through booksellers or by contacting:

Archway Publishing
1663 Liberty Drive
Bloomington, IN 47403
www.archwaypublishing.com
1 (888) 242-5904

ISBN: 978-1-4808-3690-7 (SC)
ISBN: 978-1-4808-3691-4 (HC)
ISBN: 978-1-4808-3689-1 (e)

Print information available on the last page.

Archway Publishing rev. date: 12/20/2016

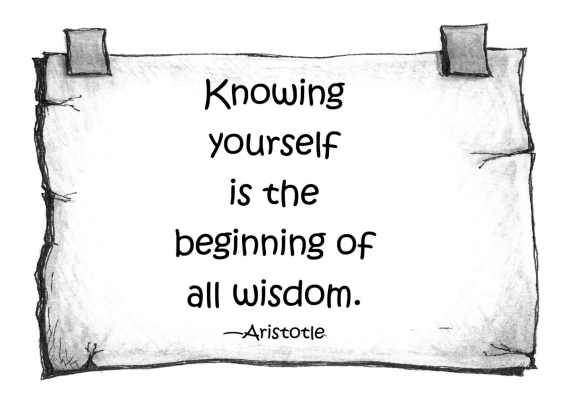

Knowing
yourself
is the
beginning of
all wisdom.
—Aristotle

Dedicated to
all our awesome
grandkids
Who have a
very weird
grandpa.

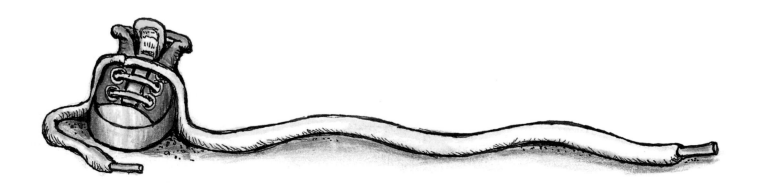

"Will you *ever* grow up?"
My schoolteacher roared.

I had been giggling and wiggling,
and feeling quite bored.

1

She tapped her foot sharply
and let out a sigh.
"I really don't know,"
was my timid reply.

My schoolteacher's name is
good ole Ms. Howell,
And most of the time
I think she's my pal.

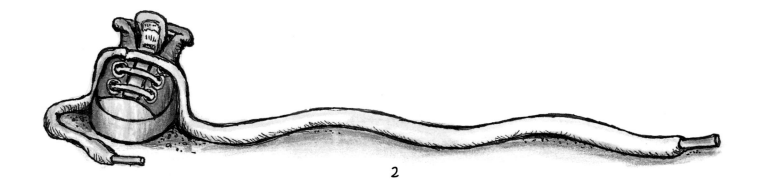

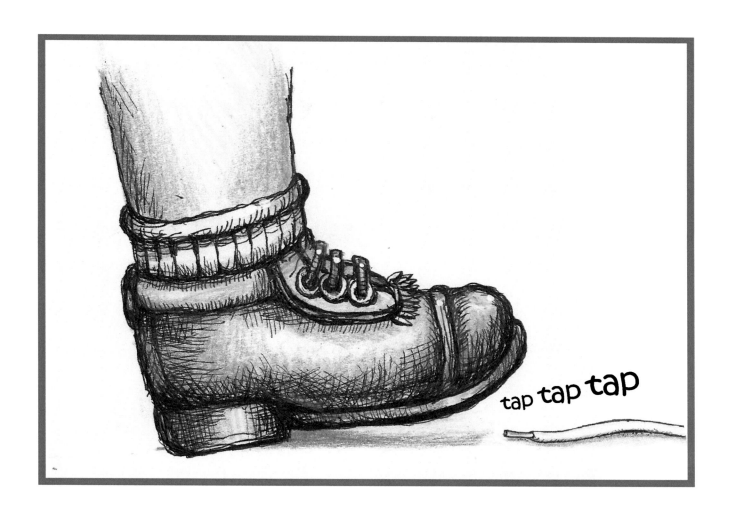

But today she got mad
because I'm so small.

So I started to think ...

Will I grow *up* at all?

And if I grow up,
then what will I be?

I really don't know ...
and it's SCARY to me.

And if I grow up,
would I still be so bad?
And then would Ms. Howell
still get so mad?

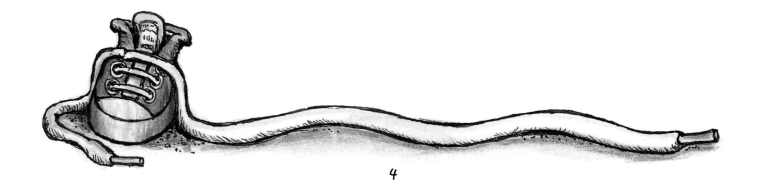

Yeah, I need to grow up.
I just don't know how.
And what will I be?
I need to know *now*.

So I looked out the window
and thought really hard.

I want to grow big,
like that tree in the yard.

"You've grown like a weed,"
my grandpa had said.

Well ... I'd much rather be
that big tree instead.

So I stood really tall
on top of my chair.
And I held up my arms;
waved them high in the air.

And my feet grew real strong,
just like roots in the ground.
But Ms. Howell gasped loudly,
"Sam, please just sit down!"

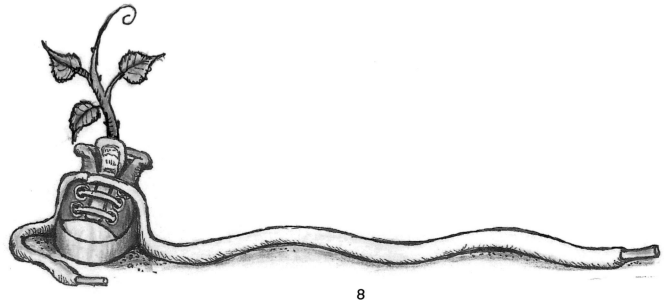

I flopped down and
Changed back into me.

But teacher's still mad.
Now what should I be?

Mmmm.

How about growing big,
mean, and gruff?
I'll grow into something
that's *strong*,
and that's *tough*.

Then I could say,
"Teacher, I've had enough.
I am a *monster!*
Grrrr, ssnort, and
rrrruffffff!"

And the kids
Would all
Shiver

And the kids
would all
Shake

And I could eat anything—
candy or cake!

So I started to moOaann,
and I started to ggrrOWll.

"Be quiet, young man!"
said an angry Ms. Howell.

"Oh, can't you be good,
like sweet little Ann?
She's such an
angel.
Be like her if you can."

Ann is an angel?
She's sweet, and she's pure?

If Ms. Howell likes Ann,
I'll just become her.

So I closed my eyes,
and I started to chant.
Well, I tried being good
but apparently can't.

Ms. Howell scurried over,
her face turning **red,**
and I probably shouldn't
repeat what she said.

Ann looked me over,
First up and then down.
She stuck out
her tongue
Then gave me a frown.

"HHhhMMMffFFF!"

If I could grow wheels,
then I could flee.
I'd drive off and never
return. Then she'd see.

"Why are you honking?"
asked my teacher, wide-eyed.

"'Cause I'm a big truck,"
I honked in reply.

But if I drove off,
I think I'd be **sad**
without any friends
or my mom or my dad.

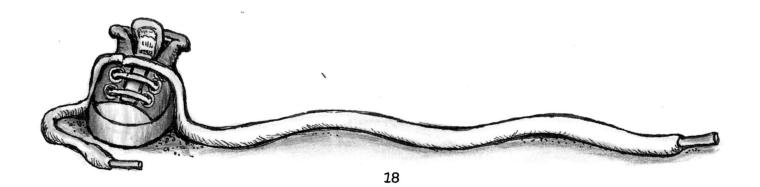

I don't like feeling sad,
But some days I do.
My smile stays in bed
Like it's got the flu.

Oh boy, I thought,
and felt suddenly glad.

I know what I'll be ...

I'll grow up
to be
Dad!

'Cause Dad and me
are alike ... well,
almost.
We both love TV,
and we both love ...

Burnt toast!

But Mom loves toast soft.
And I have to admit
I love it, too,
with some jam spread on it.

So really, in some ways,
I'm more
like another.
Maybe, just maybe,
I'll grow up
to be
Mother.

I came from her tummy
and learn lots from her,

and she tucks me in.
I'll be Mommy for sure.

Wait just a minute ...
If I'm in my bed,
and she's sitting there, smiling
and kissing my head ...

then
who
is she kissing?
Who is *that* boy
who lies in his bed with his favorite toy?

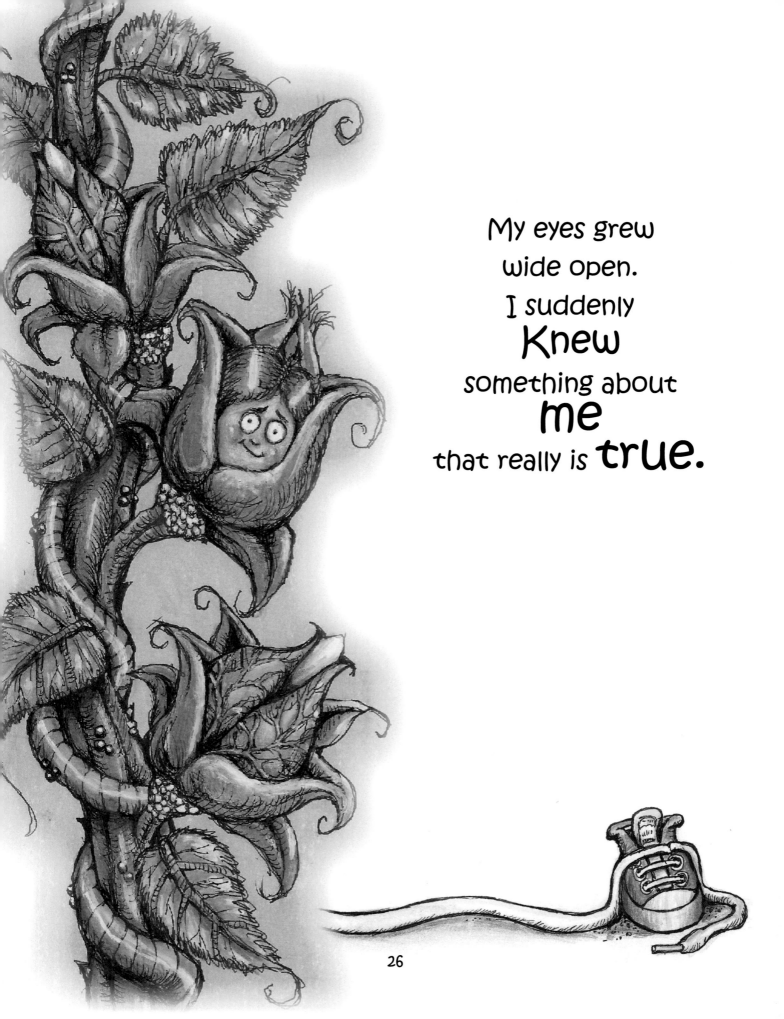

My eyes grew
wide open.
I suddenly
Knew
something about
me
that really is **true.**

26

I won't be a monster,
   all scary and bad.
But I do have some days
   when I get kinda mad.

And I won't be an angel;
I don't have to be Ann.
But my mom and dad say,
"Be as good as you can."

And I won't be a truck,
   but I can run strong.

And I won't be a weed;
Guess Grandpa is wrong.

And I won't be a tree,
'cause I'm kinda small.
But I'm gonna grow up
and get kinda tall.

So guess what I learned?
And guess what I see?

When
I grow
up,
I
will
be ...

Me!

I will be me.

Yippee!

Partly Mom's boy,
and partly Dad's son,
but mostly just me.
I am someone.

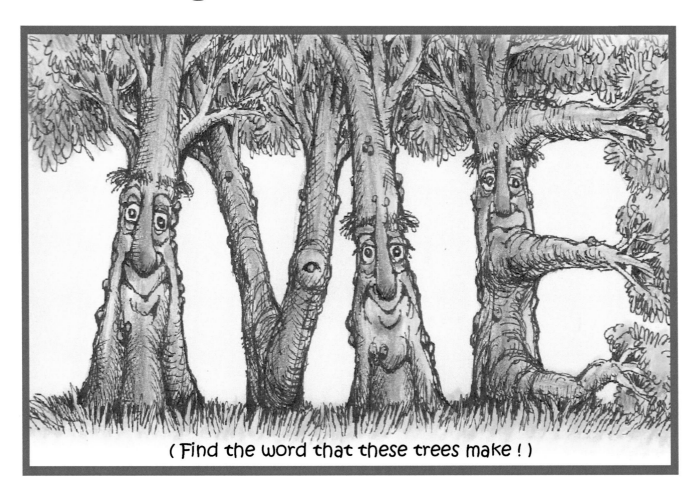

(Find the word that these trees make !)

Now that I've found me,
there are things I don't like.
My cheeks are too chubby,
and I don't have a bike.

But that is okay,
'cause I love who I am.
There's only one me,
and my name is Sam.

Some kids may just say
I am dumb and
should hide.
But I'm gonna keep being
The **me** who's inside.

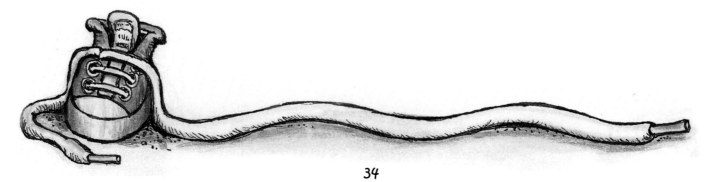

And ...
I really love Grandpa,
But there's something he needs.

I gotta tell Grandpa
we don't become weeds.

I'm gonna keep growin
and changin, it's true.
A zillion years later,
I'll finally be through.

So thank you, Ms. Howell,
for asking today,
"Will you ever grow up?"
Well, I'm on my way!

"Oh you are the best teacher I ever saw.
If only you could have taught my grandpa."

"So, I made you this picture,
'cause you helped me think.
Ms. Howell, can I go out ...
and get me a drink?"

Ms. Howell had been listening;
her eyes had been closed.

She put on her glasses
and then scratched her nose.

She studied my picture;
it took her a while.

"Hurry right back,"
she said ...

with a smile.

The end.

Will You Ever Grow Up?

Words and music by Jay Steineckert
Copyright March 2016
Accompanying the book:

I Gotta Tell Grandpa

"Will you ever grow up," my teacher asked me.
"Will you ever grow up at all?"
"Will you ever grow up or just forever,
You're always gonna be this small?"
I am just a little kid, and I don't
really get how life goes.
So when teacher asks me questions like,
"Will you ever grow up?"
I don't know.
Will I ever grow up? Well, yes I will.
I'm growin' up, yes indeed.
Yea, I'm gonna grow up.
And I gotta tell Grandpa
I'm never gonna be a weed.
I am just a little kid right now,
But every day I grow some more.
So when teach asks me questions like,
"Will you every grow up?" Yes, I'm
gonna grow up. For sure!

Coupon: for free
song download:
Go to Igottatellgrandpa.com
And type in this code: 3776

Workbook
You can use this book to teach about self-identity.

1. What are three things you like about yourself?

YOU can use this book to teach you about being you

4. Write down one way you can help your family and one way they can help you.

2. What are three things you don't like about yourself?

5. Write down two times when you felt really happy and two times when you felt really sad.

3. If you had three wishes, what would you wish for?

Draw Two Pictures.

1. Who you are right now.

2. Who you will be in ten years.

Now share your answers and pictures with someone who loves you.

Dear Friends and Parents,

Little children gather up ideas and feelings about themselves as they go about their busy days. Sometimes they pick up true ideas and real feelings about their genuine and growing selves. This is very good. But sometimes they gather up ideas and feelings about themselves that may not reflect who they really are. These seeds are planted each day in the soil of their fertile young hearts and heads. There they sprout and grow and weave together deep inside where they become fragile vessels called self-identity.

Kids use these newly built internal vessels to navigate out onto the great and scary sea of life, where they fight waves and storms, and monsters of the sky and of the deep. Some of these internal vessels turn out to be built strong and true, and hold up well through the storms of life. But many are not so strong. These vessels can get swamped with waves or broken by the battle, and then need some repair, understanding, healing and love.

So begins the journey to the self.

Remember, you will find some flaws and wounds and bandages inside. We all have them, so do not be disappointed. Every person you have ever met or will meet is also wounded in some way. Some know their wounds, and some do not. Some want to be someone else. Knowing and understanding the weaknesses and flaws in yourself and then in others and loving still, loving more, is true love.

So I offer you and your loved ones all the love in the world as you go on this most important journey to find and love and be your true self.

Love,

Jay Steineckert

To know what you prefer, instead of humbly saying "amen" to what the world tells you you ought to prefer, is to keep your soul alive.

—Robert Louis Stevenson

I am every age that I have ever been.

—Madeleine L.-Engle

There is just one life for each of us ... our own.

—Euripides

The more you like yourself, the less you are like anyone else ... which makes you unique.

—Walt Disney

It is the chiefest point of happiness that a person is willing to be who they are.
—Desiderius Erasmus

Most people are other people. Their thoughts are someone else's opinions, their lives a mimicry, their passions a quotation.
—Oscar Wilde

It is one of the most beautiful compensations in life that no man can sincerely try to help another without helping himself.
—Ralph Waldo Emerson

Printed in the United States
by Baker & Taylor Publisher Services